A WHIMSICAL JOURNEY
THROUGH THE NORTH OF SPAIN

First Published in Great Britain 2025 by Mirador Publishing

Copyright © 2025 by Terence FitzSimons

All rights reserved. No part of this publication may be reproduced or transmitted, in any form or by any means, without permission of the publishers or author. Excepting brief quotes used in reviews.

First edition: 2025

Any reference to real names and places are purely fictional and are constructs of the author. Any offence the references produce is unintentional and in no way reflects the reality of any locations or people involved.

A copy of this work is available through the British Library.

ISBN: 978-1-917411-49-3

A Whimsical Journey
Through the North of Spain

Terence FitzSimons

As It Started

I SAT BACK AND EYED the bottle of wine. I also admiringly looked at Jane. She was tall, slender, red-haired and blue eyes. What was there not to admire?

She had set her heart on persuading me to travel to Spain. "You need to get out and about. You cannot just stay here and rot in Ballarat."

Rot in Ballarat? I thought that a little harsh. "I enjoy myself here," I protested.

"Oh, come now," pressed Jane. "You really would find Spain fascinating." She paused and frowned. "And you don't have to worry about walking." She waved her empty glass.

"Sorry," I exclaimed. "I'm proving a poor host." I poured Jane a generous glass.

She took a sip of the rather expensive white wine I'd laid on and nodded her approval, but she was quickly back to the subject. "Travel in Spain would be easy for you. Trains, buses, or taxi if you wanted. You could also walk a little." This was said with a smile.

Yes, trains and buses I can deal with, the walking would be something of a problem. Bad knees had finally caught up with me. Too much rugby, soccer, and all that sort of thing in my youth. But then, I supposed I could manage a kilometre or two.

"Just how far did you walk, when you were in Spain?" I asked.

"Oh, I did a journey from Pamplona to Santiago," came the reply. "That was all of 700 kilometres. I was on the Camino de Santiago."

"That's too bloody much for me," I said as I now reached for the bottle of wine. It was rather early for me to turn to alcohol, but waste not, I thought to myself, as I found a glass and poured a generous measure.

"I assure you I'd not walk ... how far did you say?"

"Oh, 700 kilometres or thereabouts," came the casual reply. "There are some terrific places to visit there." She paused. "Even though I was a pilgrim."

A pilgrim indeed! And an attractive one too. But that was by the by, wasn't it? I took a swig of my expensive wine. "I must admit what you've told me to date, well, it all sounds very interesting." It was my turn to pause. "Not that I go for this 'pilgrim' business."

We both laughed.

"So, you'll make the trip to Spain?" asked Jane raising an eyebrow.

I felt another swig of wine was called for. "I really don't know." I sat with bowed head for a moment. "Look, I have to admit what you told me earlier, well, I find it interesting…"

"Enticing," pushed Jane.

"Maybe," I allowed. "You know I'm interested in all things historical, social history, architecture and such?"

"Yes, I know this," responded Jane.

"Ah, but you were up north."

"There's history all over the place," laughed Jane. "You could start wherever you wanted. But, if I were you I'd be inclined to spend more time up amongst the Galicians, Basques..." She was counting off the names on her fingers.

"Enough," I cried out. "Let's just say I'll have a think about a trip to Spain." I quickly refilled her glass.

It had been some while since I'd taken myself on a trip. In the early years Africa had beckoned, and that was a continent some distance from my home in Ballarat – the onetime gold mining centre of Australia – for those who have not heard of the place. But then Spain was even further afield. Nowadays I knew myself not to be the greatest of travellers. Spain? I'd have to think about it.

Better still, why not have a word with Clive Bannerville? He was a travel agent I trusted, a man who knew his way around the business of overseas jaunts. I could rely on him to see me right. 'Bannerville Best for Travel', wasn't that how he billed his business?

Up to the time of the Covid pandemic, Clive had operated from a spacious shop-front office up at the north end of MacArthur Street. But the pandemic had seen his business fall off.

As a result, he had moved himself from his expensive place of work to a tight little upstairs office in the centre of Ballarat.

Still, I had always found Clive to be adept and knowledgeable. What could he tell me about Spain, should I finally decide to travel?

Clive's relocated office was neat and, I suppose the word is 'snug'. I sat in a comfortable chair up against his desk.

This pandemic business had taken it out of him. He had put on a considerable degree of weight. I suppose you would properly classify the man now as portly. This wasn't the only physical change brought on by the tightness of business over the past years. His head of wavy dark hair had given way to a bald pate. I suppose it was by way of compensation that Clive how sported a beard, cut square so as not to obscure the bow tie which he had always sported – perhaps more as a trademark than a fashionable preference.

"Spain is it? And up north?" Clive tugged at an ear for a moment. "Up north is all well and good," he declared with a nod of his head. "But if you're going to travel to Spain, well, that far…" He sniffed. "Well in your case…"

He was gracious enough not to mention my age. Or my walking stick.

"I'd be inclined to start out from Barcelona, then I suggest you go across to Madrid." He paused and rubbed the back of his neck. "You know, see all the sights. Take your time. Then you could go for your ramble up north...if you felt like it." He stared at me. "Agreed?"

I nodded. I supposed I'd nothing to lose if I were to make a long journey out of this jaunt to Spain. Then there was the fact that I'd be travelling in July. July was not the best of times to be in Ballarat. The council, in its wisdom, had declared the city would celebrate 'Christmas in July'. Truth to tell, there was the occasional fall of snow during that month. The warmth of a Spanish July beckoned. I told Clive so.

"Good," enthused Clive. "I can get you a flight right to Barcelona." He ruffled through one of his desk drawers. "Here we have it." He laid a brochure on his desk and scanned it. "There!" He pointed to the booklet. "I can get you from Melbourne to El Prat. That would leave you 15 kilometres out from Barcelona. Easy to get a bus or taxi. OK?"

"Do it," I said as I groped for my wallet and fished out my credit card.

Clive stopped what he was writing and looked up for a moment. He laid down his pen. "May I suggest you learn a phrase or two – in Spanish?" He adjusted his bow tie and waited for my answer.

"That would be helpful," I agreed.

He picked up his pen. "Good. I'll write down a phrase or two that may be of some use to you when you get there."

Later, having glanced at the brochures Clive had given to me, I decided it would be a good idea to keep a diary of my forthcoming trip. Well, at my age could I really trust my memory? That was it then! A diary of my journey to Spain it would be.

Next day I acquired a Quill A4 notebook – 200 lined pages. That should serve me well.

Barcelona

I STIRRED AND STRETCHED AS best I could. What had it been? Over twenty hours in the air consigned to what my well-travelled friends referred to as 'cattle class', though I preferred to identify it as airline economy class. You can get a drink and a snack if you are prepared to pay. That's exactly what I did.

As the aircraft made its descent to El Prat I comforted myself with the thought that security at the airport would not be as strict as the departure procedure at Melbourne where, while my bags had been swept along on a conveyor belt through what I took to be an x-ray machine, I had waved a card indicating I was wearing a heart pacemaker and could not, therefore, risk being subjected to a *magnetic* security search. That was all well and good, until a security official subjected me to a physical body search and demanded that I remove my shoes for examination!

"Why my shoes?" I asked out of curiosity.

"Bomb!" was the curt reply. I didn't ask for any further explanation.

I later told myself that it would, perhaps, have been quicker and certainly more pleasant, if I'd taken the risk and allowed myself to be subjected to that magnetic examination, pacemaker or no pacemaker. Anyway, it was too late now, the deed had been done! I got my shoes back.

As it was, my treatment when I arrived at El Prat proved more pleasant, and certainly more speedy. A nod from customs and a smile as my passport was stamped. What could be simpler than that?

Outside the terminus I hailed a taxi and was quickly transported into Barcelona city. Clive had pre-booked me into the Olivia Plaza Hotel. I was to spend my first night there, after that I had been left to my own devices.

A Whimsical Journey

The hotel proved to be close to a quaint chapel dedicated to Saint Anne and, after a decent night's sleep, and a decent breakfast the following morning – oh, I should mention rolls, jam and pastries are filling, markedly different to bacon and egg – anyway, I went and visited the chapel across the cobbled square from the hotel.

My walk across the square was illuminated by warm bright sunlight, shining from a cloudless blue sky. What a change from the greyness and chill of Ballarat. In this part of the world, at least, it was summer.

Saint Anne's is one of the oldest churches in Barcelona. It proved to be an ecclesiastical gem. What first caught my eye was the Crusaders' emblem over the main entrance. Later investigation led me to discover that this 12th century building housed the Order of the Holy Sepulchre. A stone from that edifice was displayed in a side chapel.

It appears the knights of the order still support the work of the Catholic Church in the Holy Land. I could only wish them good luck with that undertaking.

Oh, and as to that crusaders' emblem: it

consists of a large cross surrounded by four smaller crosses. I believe it is, appropriately, called the Jerusalem Cross. Isn't that something very like the flag of Georgia?

There was one last thing Clive had insisted on as he had handed me my airline ticket to Spain. "You must visit Gaudi's church while you are in Barcelona." He stopped and corrected himself. "Actually, I believe it has been declared a basilica."

Church? Basilica? I wasn't aware there was a difference. It was only later I discovered a basilica was a place of worship of particular spiritual, and historical or architectural significance. You live and learn.

Apparently Gaudi's basilica of the Holy Family is still under construction and will be for years to come. Did I really want to visit a construction site? Why not? Holiday time!

The receptionist at my hotel gave me directions as to how to get to the basilica. "It is dedicated to the Holy Family," he explained. "You will find it in the Eixample district, just outside the old city." He drew me a map.

I did my best to follow his scribbled directions as to how to get to Gaudi's building, but in the end I decided, map or no map, it was wiser, and simpler to take a taxi.

When I got to the location I found there was a very long queue which seemed to be made up primarily of tourists, which was as well since I had no Spanish save for the few phrases Clive had given me, most of which I had forgotten. And in the event, I doubted there was very little in them that would have served me as I sought entry into the basilica of the Holy Family.

As an aside, on a later, and cautious enquiry, I was informed by a gentleman, who proved to be an American, that one required a ticket for entry to the basilica. It would cost me some forty-five dollars or thereabouts. American or Australian dollars? I didn't press the matter. So, I waited in the queue to pay my money and get my ticket.

It struck me how the only people who were pushing their way through the queue – Spaniards? – were likely to be pickpockets. I shifted my wallet to my jacket breast pocket. I had been warned of this criminality.

When I finally reached it, the interior of the

basilica proved to be quite eye-catching. There was a spectacular stairway under construction and which, I was informed, would not be finished for at least another ten years. One had the feeling that Antoni Gaudi was happy to overplay his hand. Anyway, the man had died in 1926!

That evening it was back to the hotel, and diary time.

Salvador Dali was a native of Catalonia, having been born just up the road from Barcelona – so to speak. A train ride of just over an hour took me up to the museum of his art in his home town, Figures.

I must be honest and here confess that I very quickly discovered Salvador Dali gave every appearance of being in league with the late Antoni Gaudi. A visit to this museum proved to me that a little Dali goes a long way. He was prepared to work a theme to death. But, since he was a Catalonian, I was careful not to voice any criticism of his artistic work. It was a shock to see just how his work was commemorated in what could only be described as an extremely fanciful building. The artist had died in 1989. Back to Barcelona.

A late evening wander around the city showed why the place was renowned for its architecture and culture, with old medieval buildings strewn about the city centre. I had this idea that the place would look even more attractive by moonlight. That night my supposition proved to be correct. What a vibrant night time place Barcelona proved to be. Cafés, crowds and music.

I was later to learn that one did not make reference to such an establishment as a café... it was a bistro, and that was that!

However, after I had spent two days in Barcelona I decided it was time to move on to Madrid.

I put aside my diary. Had I remembered everything? I'd better write day by day, hadn't I? That way I wouldn't miss out anything important. Oh, for good intentions! Who was it said keeping a diary could bring you inner peace?

Maybe.

A Whimsical Journey

Madrid and Segovia

I TOLD CLIVE IT WOULD be in order for him to get me to Barcelona and yes, at his suggestion I would go on to Madrid. But I would make my own way there. OK? Clive settled for a shrug of his shoulders. "You're the boss. It's your trip," he allowed. Then he insisted on telling me what I should see and do when I went to Madrid. It was my turn to settle with a shrug. "I'll do my best to take in everything," I answered with a smile – disagreeing with a smile is always the best way, isn't it?

The receptionist at my hotel in Barcelona told me that a train trip to Madrid would see me there without trouble, and he added, 'safely'. And the cost would be about fifty dollars. "Australian," I asked. Doesn't anyone work in euros?

"You Australians have dollars?" I was asked. I let the matter lie. The trip would take about six hours, so I was told. So be it; off we went.

When I arrived in Madrid I was dog tired. A six-hour train trip, buffet car service not withstanding takes it out of one. At the prompting of a fellow tourist, I found myself a reservation at the Hotel Catalonia. How appropriate, considering I had just come from that place! The hotel was situated just up from the Plaza Mayor, a locale I had been told by Clive should be on my 'must see' list. So be it!

Well, I had to admit, Clive was right about the Plaza Mayor being a place to visit. The place was awash with jugglers, musicians and rambling mummers, all intent on keeping the visitors entertained. There was, of course, the inevitable multitude of tourists.

A couple came and sat at the one vacant table in the plaza, one just next to mine. The man snapped his finger to catch the waiter's attention. To my way of thinking that was a bad move – but then, who can account for upbringing, or custom? The couple clearly were foreigners – but then, so was I. Oh well!

Still, the waiter appeared and seemed to be unperturbed by the man's discourteous action. He approached with a nod and a pleasant, "Senor, senora."

"Hamburger and chips," came the demand in what sounded to me like a Russian accent.

The waiter frowned. "Qué?" he asked.

"We're Russian," snapped the man. So, I got that right.

"We want hamburgers and chips." He glanced towards his female companion. Girlfriend? Wife? Who could tell.

"Yes, that is what we want," she said by way of agreement. The same thick accent!

"Senor, senora, I am Spanish," replied the waiter. "We do not sell hamburgers and chips." Having stated this, with a bow he left the two hungry ersatz customers.

In spite of this unwelcome interlude, I enjoyed myself in the Plaza Mayor. Oh, I had, sensibly, settled for a coffee and a pastry.

In my subsequent wanderings I came across the Royal convent of the nativity. This was a 16th century building, rather plain in appearance when set against the many medieval buildings that stood in the city centre, but this indifferent exterior was offset by the spectacular splendour of the interior and the startling display of works of art.

The Convent also featured a rather gruesome bone house containing the relics of numerous holy people and, curiously, phials of the blood of Saint Januarius, his body being buried in Italy, and also the blood of Saint Pantaleon, he being buried in France.

How the blood of these two holy men, martyrs I believe, how some of their blood came to be in Madrid was not explained to me. But then, such are the wonders of the workings of the Church of Rome.

I was doing a lot of walking, but then my stout stick was serving me well. Helped by this reliable instrument I managed to get myself up the steep hill leading to the Prado Art Gallery. Once there an enthusiastic gallery guide herded me into a group of tourists he was mustering for a hike around the gallery. He managed to hold my attention for a viewing of one medieval painting before I managed to silently slip, unnoticed, away. Truth to tell, I am one of these viewers of art who operates on the basis of 'knowing what I like'. I do not appreciate being told what I should like. I suspect I am probably not alone in this particular regard!

To be honest, 'art appreciation fatigue' had set in within a very short time. The Prada was just too cavernous, and there was too much of the same. I made my exit and settled for a coffee at a nearby bistro.

Now, there was a place I had set my mind on visiting, and it had nothing to do with a 'Clive suggestion'. I knew from various reading in the past, that Segovia had a famous Roman aqueduct. I was intent on seeing it.

Segovia, a city first built in Roman times, was some ninety kilometres north of Madrid. Enquiries at my hotel established it was best to travel there by bus. Having boarded that vehicle I found myself surrounded by American tourists ... actually, there were many in this crowd who laid claim to be Canadians. Understandable enough in the political circumstances as they stood at the time!

I had earlier been gleefully told that, in Spain, I could anticipate two hundred days of clear skies. I can't recall who passed on this 'fact' to me, but if I were to take this information seriously then, as I saw it, I could anticipate one hundred and sixty-five days of rain.

When we got to Segovia it was raining. One hundred and sixty-four days to go. Where had my sunny Spain gone?

The Roman aqueduct dominated the city and proved to be as spectacular as I had hoped it would be. A massive structure, it carried water from the River Frio, which was some sixteen kilometres away from the city. In times past this water served the fountains and public baths. More importantly it provided the various homes with water. I was told that, in some instances, it still services certain houses.

I had imagined motor traffic would have been prohibited in this part of town – crashes, vibrations, all that sort of thing, but I was wrong. It seems 'the powers that be' figured no damage was being done to the ancient structure by the traffic that rumbled under it. It seems that vehicular crashes and such did not fall for active consideration. Oh, well.

Then, apart from the Roman aqueduct, there was the 12th century Alcázar Castle, a magnificent building on a crag at the edge of the city. Visitors were admitted.

Once inside the confines of the castle I was struck by the size and beauty of the interior. The Throne Room was particularly attractive, with its magnificent tapestries and furnishings. Further on in the castle was the armoury, featuring displays of ancient weapons and in particular an armoured knight on horseback. All right; the horse was stuffed!

As a finale to my visit, and though I am a victim of vertigo, I forced myself to climb to the top parapets of this fortress. Once there I was provided with wonderful views of the surrounding township – and the opportunity to plunge to my death.

A Whimsical Journey

What I had already discovered about dining in Spain was that, if one wanted decent service, it helped to play the part of a pathetic, smiling, senile old man. That was a role which I was particularly adept at playing. I found it softened the heart of the most hardened waiter. I tended to be well treated.

Upon my return to Madrid, I took myself to the Plaza Mayor for a strong nightcap. It was then the place was drenched by a sudden downpour. One hundred-and sixty-three days still to come.

But I had decided, it was now time to set off for the northern reaches of Spain. The ancient village of Roncesvalles was to be my destination.

A Whimsical Journey

Roncesvalles and Burguete-Auritz

When we had spoken, back in Ballarat, Jane had mentioned Roncesvalles as a place I should visit. A mere village but famous as the location where the French Emperor, Charlemagne, had been engaged in a battle with the Basques – and lost.

It was the receptionist at my Madrid hotel who had told me the sensible way to travel to Roncesvalles was by bus but had also cautioned it was best I go to the bus station by taxi. For one, it was too difficult to walk there, I was likely to get lost, and two, I had to be careful and on the alert for pickpockets – echoes of Barcelona. Apparently these criminals frequent bus and train stations and many an unwary traveller became a victim. Where, I wondered, do hotel staff get all this information? I thanked the receptionist for their advice and bade farewell to Madrid.

Roncesvalles was some distance north of the city and it took the bus close to five hours to get there. The pleasant chatter of the English-speaking bus driver compensated, to a degree, for the initial dreariness of the journey. We at first travelled through doleful flat land, decorated here and there with little more than the occasional gigantic windmill, and the occasional field of solar panels.

I could not help noticing how it was that the local authorities seemed to be obsessed with road building and in particular displayed a penchant for placing roundabouts at inexplicable and inconvenient places. I formed the unsettling impression that many of the local vehicle drivers had little or no idea as to how to, legally, navigate a traffic roundabout.

However, we finally arrived at Roncesvalles, without accident. The final part of the trip had taken us over a beautiful mountain range, blessed with an abundance of attractive scenery. All of this more than compensated for the initial drabness of the initial part of the journey.

On my departure from Madrid, distracted by the hotel receptionist's litany regarding pickpockets, I had neglected to arrange accommodation at Roncesvalles. However, the cheerful bus driver, aware of my predicament, suggested I could do no better than take myself off to the local pilgrims' hostel and, if I cared to wait while he off-loaded the passengers and their baggage, he would drive me the short distance to the hostel. That way I would at least have a place to sleep for the night, tomorrow was another day and I could then, if I wanted, go hunting for other accommodation. It was an offer I was happy to accept.

The hostel provided splendid sleeping quarters, and no one bothered to enquire whether or not I was a pilgrim.

The following morning, I took myself back into the village. It is a small place, and as I made my way along paved and cobblestoned roadways, I noticed there was virtually no vehicular traffic. I was told there was a small local population, but I noticed there were a large number of Camino de Santiago pilgrims passing through the village. The hostel should have alerted me to this fact. These good people, *pilgrims*, were intent on visiting the shrine of Saint Games, his relic being on display at the cathedral in Santiago.

I didn't consider myself pilgrim material. Well, let me put it another way. I'm no great walker. For me its bus, train or taxi – but you already know all that.

Speaking of pilgrims, as I sat at a small local bistro, treating myself to a coffee and brioche breakfast, the place was invaded – if that is the word – by a group of six individuals, herded by a burly, though well turned out, French guide. I don't speak French, but the accent gave him away. Tourists or pilgrims, I couldn't tell.

When they were all seated and having ordered the meal, the guide appeared to indulge in a loud, and deep, philosophical digression which, from the bewildered looks on the faces of the group, I suspect very few, if any, actually understood. Too deep for them I think. At best one or two gave an occasional grunt or nod. In the meantime, in the very short pause in his harangue, the guide helped himself to a morsel in turn from each of the group's meal. They were having trout for which they had each paid nine euros a plate. The guide had not bothered to order a meal for himself – he had no need to!

After a while of watching this self-serving display, I took myself off on a tour of the surroundings. I was intent on reaching the Church of Roland, the French hero who had been killed way back in 778. This was when the French troops, under the command of Emperor Charlemagne, had been ambushed and defeated by a horde of Basques at the grandly named Battle of Roncesvalles. I recalled having read somewhere how Roland had been dubbed 'The Flower of Chivalry'.

Despite my earlier protestation – revelation, if you will – that I was not a great walker, I set out on foot to visit Roland's memorial. I quickly discovered the Church of Roland actually went by many names. It was, in fact, a complex of various ancient buildings. A helpful attendant at this site, who fortunately spoke English, pointed me to the Chapel of the Holy Spirit where, he claimed, the bodies of the French soldiers, slain in the Roncesvalles battle were buried. I was assured it was here that the remains of the knight, Roland, were to be found.

My question, as to where exactly one could find this noble corpse, was met with a shrug. So, where exactly was Roland interred? There was no relic or commemorative statuary to be seen. So be it.

All rather disappointing, but I suppose I had achieved what I had set out to do in Roncesvalles.

Now, having committed myself to foot, with the aid of my stout walking stick I decided to carry on and head down the road to the village of Burguete, a short distance away. If the jaunt proved too much I could always get back to Roncesvalles by taxi.

I'd been told that Ernest Hemingway had stayed at the local hotel in the village. I thought a meal there would be appropriate, and it would provide me with a worthwhile anecdote for when I got back home – how many folk can claim 'I dined where Hemingway dined'? And I could perhaps even stay the night in the place.

With all of this in mind, I set off through the local forest leading to Burguete. It was only when I reached the end of the trail that I came across a plaque informing me that I had just walked through the Witches' Forest where, during the fifteen hundreds, a number of ladies had been burnt at the stake. They were deemed to have formed a witches' coven, and in consequence had been sentenced to death. Oh, how times have changed! I later heard that the ladies in question were doing no more than collecting herbs and leaves for medicinal purposes.

All that aside, the Burguete Hotel was able to provide me with a bed for the night. The receptionist confirmed that Hemingway had indeed stayed there. What I didn't know was that the author was a keen fisherman and the local waterway, the Irati River, was rich in trout. Those fish again.

Now that he had an audience, the

receptionist told how part of the novel, *The Sun Also Rises*, was written while Hemingway was staying at the hotel. How he would have known this I couldn't say, but I let the matter lie.

The following morning, I returned to Roncesvalles by taxi. I'd done with walking for the moment, and in the event, there was no way I was heading back through the Witches' Forest. When I arrived, I enquired how best to get to Pamplona. I was promptly told by a fellow tourist that I had already passed that place. How had I managed to do that?

"Okay. Can you tell me how best I can get there?" I wanted to know.

"Well, Pamplona is south of here," I was informed. "It is about forty-seven kilometres down the road." He paused and looked at my walking stick. "You could always get a bus," was his helpful suggestion.

I thought I'd done with the fellow as he walked away but after a few paces he stopped and came back to me. "Before you go anywhere else…"

"Pamplona," I added helpfully.

"Whatever, but you mustn't leave here until you've seen the virgin's statue."

This piece of information caused me to make enquiries, as a result of which I discovered there were *two* Virgins. Both statues were brought to Roncesvalles by shepherds. One Virgin was apparently carried all the way from Lourdes, and she served as the shepherds' protector as they made this long journey. She also had a hand in looking after the sheep.

Apparently, the other statue was found by a local shepherd after he had been directed to the statue by a deer. Shepherds to the fore!

I discovered that, certainly, a statue of the Virgin Mary could be seen if I were to visit the Church of Santa Maria. This church turned out to be a rectangular building of no particular architectural merit, and it is divided into three naves, but the statue of the Virgin is a most decorated and a beautiful piece of art, with the infant Jesus seated on his mother's knee. I doubted if this work of art was in any way connected to the above mentioned shepherds. Still, I had to settle for what I'd been told by the locals.

A Whimsical Journey

Pamplona and Puente La Reina

IT PROVED VERY EASY TO get a bus from Roncesvalles to Pamplona. And I was ever mindful of the danger of pickpockets at the bus station, but they didn't present a problem. On board the vehicle, however, I found myself seated next to a stout, bald and enthusiastically verbose English gentleman. He kept up a constant chatter and kept pestering me with questions as to why I was not going to walk the Camino de Santiago. That was something he was going to do and was thrilled by the prospect of meeting fellow pilgrims along the way. With his size and obvious weight how was he going to manage all those kilometres?

Despite my assurances that I was only up north to see the sights he kept on about the Camino. I desperately looked about the bus seeking a vacant seat as far away from this enthusiastic Brit as I could get. The bus was full. I was stuck with this pilgrim!

Even with a goodly number of stops along the way the trip to Pamplona thankfully took less than an hour. When we arrived at the bus station I quickly disembarked and set as much space between myself and the would-be English pilgrim as I could manage.

There was a gift kiosk at the station, and it was there I headed and took to browsing, head well down. While I was there it struck me just how useful it would be if I got myself a guidebook. It could well go some way to helping me avoid the debacle I had initially experienced in overshooting Pamplona and heading for Roncesvalles!

To date I had been operating on hearsay from Jane and Clive back in Ballarat. I purchased the book. There was bound to be something regarding hotel accommodation in this publication.

The trip into the city had already given me

the idea that this was not a small place, certainly a darn sight larger than Roncesvalles. I later learnt that it had a population of over 200,000, a lot bigger that Ballarat.

Reference to my newly acquired guidebook directed me to the Casa Otano. I quickly booked into this modest hotel in the city centre. I was getting use to the idea of being a simple tourist and certainly not a pilgrim. So it was, as a tourist, I took a walk through the city and finished up at the Church of San Cernin, a fortress-like building.

When I arrived there I was promptly directed towards the statue of Our Lady of the Camino. That *pilgrim* stuff again! But the statue was a delight to behold, but I was told she had made a miraculous appearance in the church rafters some 500 years ago. I was given 1478 as the date of this miracle.

It was not only the virgin in the rafters business that got me thinking, but there was, at the west end of the church, some remarkable flowing. It consisted of slabs of wood, each I reckoned, at over a metre long and some eight centimetres wide or so. It you went by the old measurements, as I do, you'd work that out at something like four and a half feet by two and a half feet. Each large timber slab was numbered and was fitted with a rebated metal handle at one end. This presumably was to allow for the easy lifting of the slab, but to what purpose? The whole thing remained a mystery. Certainly the few English speakers I approached and asked about the floor were as baffled as I was as to the purpose of these slabs.

Earlier, as I walked through the city, I had been bemused by the mingling of high-rise buildings mixed in amongst medieval structures. In many instances these old buildings were not the small structures I'd come to expect by rather palatial edifices.

Come to think of it the Church of San Cernin had a *defensive* look about it. Later I was told that the towers of the church were used as look-out posts in defence of the city. I recall how in the past I had come across similar *stone* slabs, not timber ones, inserted in cloisters. Maybe the slabs I saw had something to do with defence. Ah, I suspect these things will always remain mysterious!

In the evening, I decided to have a drink in the Café Iruna, an establishment just off the Plaza del Castillo in the centre of the city. Once again it turned out to have been a haunt of Ernest Hemingway. There is a life-sized statue of the author propping up the Iruna bar next to the café. It has been a long time since I read *The Sun Also Rises*, but unless I'm mistaken, it was at this bar that the book's main character, Jake Barnes, went to drink.

I recalled that Hemingway was a keen fisherman and the rivers hereabouts are homes to many varieties of trout. Unfortunately for the would-be angler the city's waterway, the Arga, is not the best of places for fishing; there are many picnic sites and walkways all along the banks of the river.

Oh, as an aside, the hotel keeper here is a very pleasant gentleman. I found it curious, but attractive, that he had an accent just like Manuel in *Fawlty Towers*. But then, maybe, there are many too young to remember that television series.

As a tourist, I should warn would-be travellers, that the Spanish – or at least the Basques – seem to have an aversion to hot shower water. Or maybe it had something to do with the time of year I was making my visit – July. Maybe the locals considered it hot enough at this time of year to forgo the luxury of hot shower water! However, it was difficult to find a reasonable sized bath. This particular washing facility, when one comes across it, appears to be best suited for a dwarf, or a yoga contortionist. Oh, while on the subject of hot and cold, I arrived in Spain, minus a hat Silly! I had to do something about that. My head and ears were taking a beating from the sunny conditions … two hundred days was it?

All that washing and sun business aside, the following morning I planned to visit the Citadel. The place is an old military fortress, though it no longer serves that purpose. It now consists mainly of a number of abandoned moats, drawbridges and the ruins of fortifications. Supposedly the place was designed to protect the city from external

A Whimsical Journey

aggression, but local history indicates that the place did little to suppress or control internal riots and disturbances.

The original pentagon defence, copied from the Dutch, was massive and convoluted. It was unclear to me just what defensive attributes one could have credited the structure with. Obviously, it would have required the presence of a very large garrison force. Whatever the situation, it did not deter the French from attacking and capturing the fort.

If my memory serves me, the city suffered this defeat during the Peninsular War of 1808, or thereabouts. The fortress ruin had been declared a National Monument.

I found myself walking a great deal, and in this regard my sturdy walking stick proved to be an invaluable aid. This being so, I decided I was ambulatory enough to make my way to the Church of Saint Nicholas. The church is a 12th century building, and I was informed it was worth a visit to view the statuary displayed there.

The church proved to be a beautiful compact building, and all the statues were painted in striking colours, which I took to reflect a singular medieval style.

A magnificent central altar stood at the head of the nave, without the distraction of side chapels. In many of the other churches I had visited a multiplicity of side chapels, some caged, had detracted from the overall devotional aspect of these ecclesiastical buildings.

Later I made my way to inspect the local bullring, but I found it closed. Apparently it is not considered a tourist attraction – that to my way of thinking is a good thing! Anyway, whatever the reason, the locals do not make the place readily accessible to tourists and I, for one, must admit I wanted to see the place merely out of curiosity.

There is an annual 'running of the bulls', where the poor beasts gallop through the streets, impeded or encouraged by the locals. I missed that affair by a week – anyway, I'm for the bulls!

A Whimsical Journey

But now, having brought up the subject, as I recall it a Spanish bullfight ends with the demise of the bull, dispatched in the ring by the matador. Personally, I believe the Portuguese option is better, with the bull freed at the end of the 'fight' to feed in pastures.

By now my ramblings took me off to the city wall, down by the River Arga. I had set myself to once again visit the church of Saint Nicholas. Why had I decided on a second visit? Well, I had found the colourful statues most attractive, and the centrality of the altar was striking. *Centrality,* is that the right word?

On returning to my hotel, I enquired of the *pleasant* hotel keeper if there were any other local places I should visit. Well, if I were prepared to go a little further afield, he would recommend a trip to view the Punta la Rena, which he helpfully translated as the Queen's Bridge. It was just twenty kilometres down the road and there was a regular bus service.

The following morning, after a good breakfast, a few glasses of wine, and detailed instruction and a sketched map, from mine host, I found the bus station without too much difficulty. It was apparent that medieval town designers didn't have much time for 'grid' set outs. There was every appearance about these old places that they just came about, piece by piece so to speak. The sketch map proved most helpful.

Having arrived at the bus station and boarded the bus bound for Punta la Rena the departure of the vehicle was delayed. This occasioned a loud, and what I took at the time to be abusive, argument, between the passengers and the driver of the vehicle. All this had occurred on the heels of an announcement that the bus's departure was being delayed pending the arrival of postal material destined for Punta la Rena.

To be honest the nature of this whole argument was primarily supposition on my part since the only word I could claim to understand was 'correspondencia' – but that was not too difficult to work out.

After a delay of some twenty minutes a bedraggled elderly gentleman, who gave no appearance of having anything to do with the postal service, arrived. In turn he greeted the bus driver and when he had saluted all the other passengers he took a seat at the rear of the bus. The driver immediately engaged gear and drove off!

What was all this postage business? Had I got it wrong? Suffice it to say I was satisfied finally to be underway.

I've probably referred to Puente La Reina as a town – let me correct that – it is a village with a population of 2,900 souls. Our bus stopped outside the village since it is impossible for 'bus size' vehicles to travel through the village, the streets in places are so very narrow. Access to the village centre is through a series of laneways, no more than a small car in width. When such a vehicle approaches, as few do, then everyone gets off the street and into doorways.

The bridge I'd travelled to see was a beautiful 11th century structure. The story has it that the edifice was built on the orders of Queen Muniadona, wife of King Sancho III. And, if you believed it, the bridge was built to ease the way for pilgrims travelling to Santiago. That Camino business again.

There is another tale also told concerning

the bridge. Some of the old locals have contended that it was not so much intended as an ease for pilgrims, but rather it was constructed as a successful endeavour to increase local business. The place had previously been devoid of anything in the way of local industrial or agricultural focus. Whatever. The locals had benefited.

That evening, when I returned to Pamplona, as I sat in the bar finishing my second glass of refreshing wine, I witnessed the boisterous arrival of six ladies. Immediately their accents identified them as Irish. It wasn't long before I got into conversation with this interesting group. It transpired they were all Dubliners, and cousins to boot. They had pledged themselves to walk the Camino de Santiago, but with the proviso they would only visit the Camino annually, and each time walk one hundred kilometres. This was their first outing.

I asked if they realised the distance from Pamplona to Santiago was some seven hundred kilometres? At one hundred kilometres a year? Seven years! My question was greeted with laughter and nods of assurance.

Good luck ladies.

On my last day in Pamplona, I took a final ramble through the city. I was becoming quite conditioned to walking, aided of course by my stick. There were still a number of sights to see, though probably the most striking was the old Town Hall – city Hall, if you will. The building is a magnificent three-storied affair, balconied and crested with its summit adorned with statues. All this left me personally excited. A colourful 14th century structure! We had nothing to match it at home.

I next took myself to the Plaza del Castillo, the central square in the heart of Pamplona. This plaza is blessed with a multiplicity of cafés (should that be bistros?). Some would claim there is a surfeit of these establishments. A beautiful domed bandstand features in the centre of the plaza.

Overcome by it all, I settled for a few

brandies before returning to my hotel. Tomorrow would see on my way to my new destination: Obanos.

A Whimsical Journey

Obanos and Eunate

BY THIS STAGE IT HAD already become clear that the guidebook I had acquired in Pamplona could well prove helpful on my further journey across the north of Spain. Prior to my departure from Pamplona, I had scanned the booklet's contents and settled on the village of Obanos as my next port of call. Curiously this place was not too far from the Puente La Reina.

Obanos boasts a population of 900 inhabitants, and the village is renowned for its presentation of the mystery play which told of the murder of Saint Felicia and her brother Guillen.

Being only twenty kilometres away from Pamplona I decided to walk to Obanos. I was proving adept at this pedestrian business, particularly since I could rely on my walking stick for support and, though still hatless, I looked forward to a sunny walk to my destination.

That was all well and good, except I had overestimated my prowess as a walker and arrived exhausted at my destination and, to top this, I hadn't allowed for the fact that my mid-day arrival found just about all the locals enjoying their siesta.

Solitarily, I wandered around and passing a church – closed – I saw fluttering on the noticeboard an old pamphlet, informing me, in English, that the performance of the mystery play was 'scheduled for June'. So much for that entertainment!

A further reading of the guidebook revealed the same church held the skull of Saint William encased in a silver bust of the holy man. On the ninth of May each year wine and water are poured over the skull and the locals gather to drink this supposedly beneficial brew. Quaffing the mixture is said to ensure good health and, possibly, cure any specific ill oppressing the recipient. Ninth of May? Well, I'd *missed* that and the mystery play.

Again the guidebook proved helpful. It told me Punta la Reina was only four kilometres away. I walked.

On arrival I booked in at the Hotel Rural Bidean, an old brick building but very comfortable for all that. I was settling in for a drink, or two, at the hotel bar when I was greeted by the six Irish cousins I had earlier encountered at Pamplona. They arrived at the hotel seeking refreshments. They proved to be enthusiastic drinkers of the local wine. They were in good form, and voice, having completed the first one hundred kilometres for the Camino de Santiago. Only some six hundred kilometres to go. Good luck, ladies! They informed me they were on their way back to Pamplona by bus, onward to France then back to Dublin. I was sure they would have scintillating tales to tell – to anyone who was prepared to listen!

The next day, having been prompted by the Irish ladies, I went out to Eunate to visit the church of Saint Mary. While the location was only some seven and a half kilometres away, I decided to travel by bus. I'd had enough walking for the moment.

The history of the church, as with many other structures in Spain, was the subject of debate between two opposing parties. I suppose this is really a common enough occurrence, and I am probably wrong in attributing it singularly to the Spanish. Anyway, one group stoutly declared the place to be a Templars' chapel, while the opposition holds it is simply a funeral chapel.

I did seem to be spending a lot of time visiting churches but, Templar or funereal, I found Saint Mary's attractive, and I noticed a singular number of masons' marks displayed on the stonework of the building.

Ballarat sports a number of such marks on early erected stone bridges and the occasional lined channel. Proud of my discovery I pointed out the marks to a fellow tourist. This information was greeted with a nod, and I was informed that there was a display and explanation of such marks to be found on a monument on a hill not far from the chapel. How did he know that? I took the bus back to

A Whimsical Journey

Puente La Reina. I had planned a journey to Estella for the next day.

Estella

DESTINATION ESTELLA. I WAS TRAVELLING without having made any prior arrangements regarding accommodation, but that proved no problem. Arriving in Estella I easily booked a room in an hotel overlooking the Plaza de los Fueros. I quickly got myself down to the plaza which is at the city centre and is a general meeting place for the citizens Estella. And true to its reputation, the place was alive with people and awash with musicians. I ordered a bottle of red wine at one of the bistros and sat down to enjoy the music. It was then, as I gazed around, that I noticed one side of the plaza was taken up by a relatively modern building. When I enquired I was told the building was actually the Church of John the Baptist. Churches gain!

On investigation I discovered there was no easy way into the church. The main door, when I finally got to it, proved to be an unprepossessing plain wooden affair and it was firmly shut. In fact, it was being used by the local youth as a soccer goal. A large notice was attached to this door declaring *Soy Eskizofrenic*. It was only on my return to Ballarat, and checking on Google Translate on my computer, that I discovered whoever had placed the notice on the church door was declaring 'I am schizophrenic'. What was all that about?

Referring again to that guidebook of mine it told me how the township had initially been highly populated by Jews, but that group had been expelled in 1498. Did I really need to know that?

It is perhaps understandable how churches had become a particular feature to this northern part of Spain. The Moors, in their time, had exercised control of a great portion of the southern portion of the peninsula.

While in Estella I set myself to visit the Church of Santa Maria Jul del Castillo. No, I was not becoming totally obsessed with visiting churches. This place had been converted to serve as an interpretation centre. Originally the church had been built on the ruins of a synagogue following a massacre of the local Jews in the early 14th century. That guidebook again!

The centre itself, while proving to be an attractive building, was something of a disappointment since the material housed there tended to relate, in greater part, to matters concerning the civil war. Ballarat's Eureka revisited, if you will.

No, I best be fair. I did discover the XP symbol which I had increasingly noticed on buildings all about, was the *chi rho* – the *alpha* and *omega*, if you will. It served to distinguish buildings inhabited by Christians as distinct from those used by Jews and Muslims.

A little depressed, having been disappointed by the contents on display at the interpretation, I took myself to the Museo Gustavo de Maeztu – again an entry in *that* guidebook, but in this instance back home I had actually heard of this artist. I was not disappointed by the wonderful colourful works by this man.

Material at the Museo left me understanding that the artist had been born back in 1887 in the city of Vitoria, situated to the north of Estella and he had died here, in Estella, in 1847. My personal response to the work of this artist is that it stands streets ahead of the material produced by Salvador Dali, whose works I had viewed down in Barcelona.

I had been told of a monastery just up the road that produced a very fine wine and – this was the attraction – the establishment featured an external wine fountain. You could get a free glass of wine from this contraption.

It was at two kilometres out from Estella. That walking stick again. I went and had some free wine, and at the same time discovered that the Benedictine monks no longer occupied the (now so-called) monastery. Apparently it had been taken over by a wine manufacturing concern in the nineteen hundreds, but they still dispensed the free wine. So, it was courtesy of the new owners that I had my draught of good, tasty red.

I decided to make an early night of it as I set my next destination as Santo Domingo de la Calzada. I intended to travel by train. So to bed.

I woke with a start. What was that noise, I asked myself? A bell, someone was ringing a bell! An early morning start of some sort? Then I realised the sound was coming from the square outside of the hotel. I went to the window to see what was going on.

I was greeted by the sight of some thirty people in the square headed by a bell-ringing portly gentleman, adorned with a red beret, scarf about his throat and carrying a lantern. As I watched the group was joined by a flautist, accordionist, a mandolin player and a guitarist. With these musicians accompanying them the group sang a beautiful song. At the conclusion of this melodious piece the bell-ringer again started his clattering and led the group out of the square.

A Whimsical Journey

Later, on my way to the train station, I came across a very tall plinth which was topped by a statue of a beret adorned figure carrying a bell and lantern. The base of this erection was adorned with emblems which meant nothing to me. Unfortunately, there was no inscription on the plinth. Clearly, there was some history behind the enactment I had witnessed – a story of some sort but as to what it was I remained clueless!

It was on this note of *mystery* I took my leave from Estella.

A Whimsical Journey

Calzada and Badaran

WHEN I ARRIVED IN SANTO Domingo de la Calzada the guidebook, which I'd got hold of in Pamplona, helped direct me to the Parador of Santo Domingo. I had early on discovered that parodores were a chain of State-owned hotels usually located in historic buildings. The one in Calzada was in a converted 12th century hospital.

I had imagined I had by now done with churches. I was wrong. The parador I had chosen overlooked the cathedral of Santo Domingo. Oh, well, we'd see about that later.

As I sat at the hotel/parador bar consuming my third glass of the splendid local red wine, I was joined – without me having extended any sort of invitation – by an Irish pilgrim. Another one? This time it was a bloke.

My uninvited companion did not have to tell me he was Irish. Tall, gaunt, pale skinned and red-headed, he spoke with a drawl just like the six lady cousins I had earlier met.

Clutching a glass of vino, he told me he didn't like to drink alone. "And you looked as if you could do with some company," he explained, with a nod towards me.

I was tempted to reply that I always found my own company sufficient and satisfactory, but I settled for returning his nod. Anyway, he had already sat himself down opposite me. He told me his usual drink was whiskey, Irish, of course, but he admitted he'd taken a fancy to the local wine. Well at least that made two of us.

Some glasses of wine later we established that I was not a pilgrim. "Be that as it may," said Seán, "you must visit the cathedral and view the cock and hen."

"A cock and hen in a cathedral?" I was intrigued.

Two matters for consideration arose from all

this conversation. Firstly Seán, having given me his name, informed me that it should be spelt with an accent over the A. I was informed that this item was called a 'fada'. So be it.

Later the realisation struck me just how frequently Spanish names sported an accent, be it a 'fada' or some other decoration. I'd already come across a José and a Gómez.

As to the second matter, Seán had already told me how the Irish loved a good story, the more fanciful the better. And the cathedral cock and hen fitted into this category and Seán was prepared to tell me this tale. He ordered more drinks for the both of us, and then there was no stopping him.

It seems that way back in the past, a family of pilgrims was passing through the township here when a local girl instantly fell in love with the couple's teenage son. However, he being a good Christian, rejected all of her advances.

The young lady, now feeling besmeared by the young man's lack of attention, secreted a silver cup in his luggage, and then accused him of theft. The local Sheriff was called and, rummaging through the lad's baggage, found the silver cup.

Taken before the local authorities, and despite his protestations of innocence, the lad was found guilty and sentenced to be hanged. The young smitten lady was satisfied – if she couldn't have him no one could.

The young man's mother and father were, obviously, distraught. They had seen their son hanging on a gibbet. They quickly formed the mistaken belief that the boy may be still alive. Acting on this assumption, they quickly approached the Sheriff and asked for the hanging boy to be released.

That gentleman was sat devouring his evening meal. "Released?" snapped the Sheriff. He objected to his meal being interrupted. He laughed derisively and gestured to a plate of roast fowls. "That lad of yours is no more alive now than these chickens I'm about to eat."

No sooner had the Sheriff said this than the fowls on the platter spouted beaks and feathers and flapped away from the dining table. Seeing this the Sheriff rushed out and had the young man cut down from the gallows. To everyone's surprise he was still alive. He was promptly pardoned and allowed to proceed with his parents on their pilgrimage.

"So, there you have it," declared Seán, as he finished the story and beckoned a waiter and ordered more wine for the pair of us. "As a result of this miraculous happening there is now a live cock and a hen kept over there in the cathedral. You should go and see them."

I promised I would do that on the morrow. With that a smiling and unsteady Seán made his way off to bed. Come to think of it, he hadn't given me his family name – for that matter, I hadn't given him my name.

The next morning there was no sign of the Irishman, but I did as I had promised. There they were! Two fowl in an ornate coop, high on one of the cathedral walls. The two birds also featured in a stained-glass window. As to the building itself it was a mishmash of ecclesiastical styles and items, all thrown together on top of each other. There was an extraordinary and very large altar piece, I reckoned it at some five metres tall and featuring many figures that I did not recognise. It was covered with enough gold to pay off some country's national debt. How disappointing.

After I left the cathedral a thought struck me. There were so many fantastic stories to be told in this part of the world, and I'd probably missed most of them to date. I mean, what was the story behind that bell-ringing and lantern carrying man back at Estella? I must smarten up.

As I stood considering my next destination I was passed by a brass band which I promptly followed to a city square. This place had a group of red scarfed locals who, on investigation, I discovered were boiling up vats of mushrooms. It turned out they were members of a confraternity which, among its other duties, looked after the cock and hen in the cathedral.

Meanwhile the brass band members took up positions on a temporary stage and, between swigging wine and scoffing mushrooms and hunks of bread, played the occasional tune.

There was a massive queue lined up to collect a serving of mushrooms and a slice of bread. It appeared most of the locals were involved in this mushroom eating business. Elderly citizens, seated in wheelchairs, were included in the press waiting to be served from the steaming vats.

What was the story behind all of this? I was left as ignorant and puzzled by all of this as I had been by the bell-ringer at Estella!

I had no Spanish, apart from the few phrases Clive had given me back in Ballarat. To be honest, I had forgotten most of them, though there were one or two I could recall. I could ask, in Spanish, 'can you help me?'. Which was all well and good, but I might not be able to understand anything that came to be said by way of assistance. But I could follow this up with 'no hablo Espanol': 'I do not speak Spanish'. Not really helpful, I suppose.

And now, in spite of the size of the gathering I was unable to find an English speaker. It had been suggested to me that most Spanish schools taught English as a second language. Clearly, not in this part of the country. Pity I'd not paid much attention to Clive's efforts.

In the long run I was left – as I still am – with no idea what this mushroom affair was all about. I was told the region is famous for its mushroom dishes, along with fiestas for various saints. Could this have been some sort of combined event? I'm as puzzled as ever!

Next stop the village of Badaran. It was about seventeen kilometres down the road from Calzada, so I took a taxi. My supply of Australian dollars was holding up very well and, at least for now, the dollar was standing up well against the euro.

Over at Badaran there were two ancient monasteries I wanted to see. One, a very old establishment, had been converted into a parador, earning itself four stars. It was down in a valley and went by the title of Parador Santo Domingo. The other monastery was a small affair up on an adjacent hill side.

To my horror I discovered the monastery,

standing on what was to prove to be a very steep hill, could only be accessed by one joining a tourist group and then, under the control of a local guide, being transported by bus up to the destination.

When I got to the bus there were close to a hundred people waiting for transport up the hill. Two bus-loads, at least!

I do suspect that the guides at Badaran were suffering from tourist overload. I'm told it is becoming quite common. Since I visited, I believe certain parts of Spain have now started levying a tourist tax. So much for *over-tourism.*

I have to admit – again – that my visit in Spain saw me spend a deal of time meandering around churches and monasteries. But then there are an awful lot of such religious establishments in the country, leastways where I was spending most of my time, up north, so, I was prepared to put up with the inescapable discomfort of being taken up to the establishment on the hill, travelling in a crowded omnibus!

On arrival at the summit there stood a small building recessed into a cliff face. A very interesting situation. Perhaps one could say, *a la Petra*? It then became a case of following the guide. Here I was immediately in trouble. I was part of a large group of Spanish tourists, and, in consequence, the guide gave all the information regarding the monastery in that language. Being ignorant of all that was being told us, I eventually took myself off to do a little private viewing.

My private investigation led me to a tiny cell, deeply recessed into the side of the hill. I permitted myself to assume the site had been the habitation of a hermit or some such recluse. It was at this stage that I came to the realisation that I was totally alone. Where had all the others got to?

I was quick to discover that the tourist bus had departed. Obviously, the guide had not counted the number of tourists who had embarked on the way up, so had no real idea that there was a missing member of the group – me!

I was left to find my way down the hill. I was fortunate in two regards: there was a pathway down to the lower reaches, granted overgrown in places, but leading down to the valley and I had my walking stick.

A Whimsical Journey

Out of curiosity I spent one night in the Parador Santo Domingo, but the place, while comfortable, I found to be very impersonal. Next morning I took my leave and whilst in the village, I found a quaint inn where I got accommodation. While the staff were happy to have me as a guest, I was cautioned that the following day's service was likely to be a little irregular as there was a festival being held on the morrow and all would be attending. Some local saint or such, I assumed, but management didn't choose to elaborate. I decided not to press the matter.

Breakfast the following morning was a simple affair: coffee, bread and jam. No wine? The waiter and the kitchen staff were all a jabber, clearly looking to the day's celebrations. And, so it happened, I was left alone in the inn while all the staff absented themselves to join in the local festivities.

Come lunchtime, with no activity in the inn's kitchen, I took myself into the village just to see what was happening. All the bistros were crowded. There was a great deal of laughter

A Whimsical Journey

and singing from the packed bistros ... and, obviously, a lot of wine was being drunk. I returned to the vacant hotel. But then there was an unattended (open) bar and a vacated kitchen. If I were to be left to my own devices, so be it.

The availability of a supply of *free* liquor proved a temptation. Here was a chance to sample the local beer. Everywhere I went I'd seen this *Estrella Galacia* brew being advertised. Here in the bar were bottles of the stuff. I took one from the shelf and carefully examined it. Dark in colour, and 5.4% alcohol per bottle. Fair enough. And the kitchen provided bread rolls, cheese and salami. After three bottles of the brew, I lay back in a lounge chair and, truth to tell, I must have dozed off.

Later that evening I was awakened by the noisy boisterous return of the staff. It was obvious they had enjoyed themselves at the local festival. Just what saint had prompted this display of cheerfulness remained a mystery.

Dinner that night was served by an unsteady, bleary-eyed waiter. I doubted the meal had been prepared in the kitchen, more likely it had been purchased at a local bistro, where someone had contrived to remain sober!

I had thought to spend the next day rambling through Badaran, but when I got to the village centre I discovered that the locals were still 'celebrating' the feast of the saint – or whatever it was they had been 'venerating' yesterday. All the watering-holes and bistros were packed, and everyone seemed to be already well into their cups. I went back to the hotel where, to my surprise, notwithstanding the staff's involvement in yesterday's high jinks, the kitchen managed to turn out a reasonable lunch. However, I was informed that dinner that night would be table – d'ote. Obviously, the kitchen staff was not yet fully recovered.

So be it. The next day I promised myself a bus ride to Burgos.

A Whimsical Journey

Burgos

THE BUS ROUTE INTO THE city of Burgos unfortunately ran through an extensive industrial site. Now, that didn't augur well for my visit. Then to add to my already dim view of matters, the hotel that the hotel keeper at Badaran had recommended was closed! After a hunt, and more by chance than design, I finished up booking a room in the Edificio Aptos Turisticos. This proved to be pleasant accommodation, and the place was overseen by a cheerful and pleasant young manager. I suppose I had to admit things were now beginning to look up.

What was that earlier comment concerning

rainy days against sunny ones? Well, I was now sorely tested by the heat and sun. I really was in need of a head covering. The popular beret worn in this region was not suitable. I had to have headwear that covered my already burnt and blistered ears.

I wandered into the older part of the city. Here everything stood in contrast to the industrial area that the bus had earlier in the day travelled through. This central area had a very continental feel about it, by that I mean it had a general European atmosphere rather than a singular Spanish one.

As luck would have it, it was in this part of the city that I came across a hat shop. The shop was a revelation, run by a *genuine* hatter. It sported a wood panelled interior with a multiplicity of bevelled mirrors and hats on display everywhere, on stands, hooks and manikin heads.

The owner was a tall, slim moustachioed gentleman. He was splendidly turned out in, what I took to be, an expensive three–piece suit. His English was perfect. He told me he had spent some years in London, 'learning the business', as he put it.

A Whimsical Journey

We searched through his stock and came up with a French Crambes hat, wide brimmed and very Harrison Ford/Indiana Jones, in style. A mere seventy-five euros. My ears, and nose, would now be well protected from the Spanish sun.

So, things were looking up? Well, not quite! I had decided to visit the cathedral in the city centre. Granted the exterior of the building was magnificent, but that was the end of it. I found the interior of this ecclesiastical establishment a great disappointment. If I were to use an unkind words to describe the place then I would use the expression, *monstrously horrible.*

Earlier I mentioned how my time to date in Spain had seen me become converted into something of a church visitor. If this cathedral of Santa Maria were any indication as to what I could expect on the remainder of my trip – then, all was going downhill!

The cathedral interior consisted of a number of caged off areas. I'd previously seen something similar, but nothing as overpowering as I witnessed here. To the left and right of the narrow ambulatory were caged side chapels. One was left with the inescapable sense that the benefactors and bishops involved in erection of these structures were more interested in memorialising themselves than catering for the spiritual and physical needs of the churchgoers.

After this episode at the cathedral, I felt in need of a strong drink. A nearby bistro, just off the Plaza Mayor, was able to supply me with a draught of my newly discovered brew, Estrella Galicia beer. I now wanted to find some way to counter my earlier disappointment. Ah, that guidebook again! Maybe I'd find some acceptable suggestion there. I did!

The book informed me that a visit to the Castillo de Burgos was an essential event to be undertaken by any visitor to the city. I discovered that the castle, a ruin, was situated on the Hill of San Miguel. It towered seventy-five metres above the city. Perhaps the old measurements will give some of you a better idea of the castle's location. How about 246 feet above the city? Well, with my new hat and walking stick I was well equipped for the climb.

When I reached the top of San Miguel I was confronted by large wooden gates which I took as being the main entrance to the castle. They were closed and apparently locked.

Having made the climb I was not to be stymied by closed gates. I used my walking stick to hammer loudly on the entrance. Eventually my loud banging was answered by a uniformed gentleman who emerged from a small door, off the side of the locked entrance. I took this man to be the castle guide.

I explained I was a visitor from Australia and would love to view the old castle. It was politely explained to me that the venue was closed, it being a Thursday. I told Abel, I later discovered this was his name, I was prepared to return on the Friday. Abel let me know Friday also saw the castle closed.

"You could visit on Saturday," he suggested.

"I intend to head for Castrojeriz on Saturday," I told him.

"I'm sorry," he said. His English was very good. He smiled. "But we old soldiers must do as we are told."

I sensed an opportunity. "You were a soldier?" I asked.

Again the smile. "A long time ago. I was a sergeant."

"I too was in the army," I told him. "I was a captain."

Abel took a deep breath and pulled back his shoulders. "A commissioned officer?"

I nodded.

"Well, I, a sergeant, cannot impede an officer!"

Impede? I liked that.

With that he glanced about. Satisfied we were alone he pulled open his little door and invited me into the castle.

I spent a very pleasant and informative hour with Abel as he guided me around the ruins. Here and there a playground had been established.

"We can get a big crowd in here on the days we are open," Abel explained. He gestured to one of the playgrounds. "Not all children are interested in these ruins."

He informed me how the French invaders,

in the year 1813, had blown up a great portion of the castle after the Spanish militia had forced them into retreat. Archaeological digs were evidently underway at portions of the old fortifications.

At the end of the tour through the castle I tried to press some Australian dollars into Abel's hand. "No, Captain," he protested, "it was a pleasure to deal with an officer."

And it was a pleasure to have dealt with such an obliging sergeant.

That evening, I decided to return to the bistro I had earlier discovered just off the Plaza Mayor. I allowed myself to be adventurous and ordered chorizo, bean and sausage soup. Excellent! Then I followed this up with a serving of the local black-pudding. I have to admit this savoury put German blutwurst in the shade, and Irish black-pudding wouldn't stand up against it at all.

On Saturday I was heading to Castrojeriz. Another castle to investigate.

A Whimsical Journey

Castrojeriz

IT WAS THE GUIDEBOOK THAT had set me up for matters military. Burgos is a case in point, and I must admit that Abel had a lot to do with showing that to be a splendid destination – that old, ruined castle, I mean, where Abel was the guide.

But you will recall, even before my visit to the ruin at Burgos I had settled on getting to Castrojeriz to view the castle there and that's where I was now.

I was informed – that guidebook again – that the castle had originally been built sometime in the ninth century. It withstood attacks from the invading Muslim forces. It was finally reduced to a ruin by an earthquake in 1755.

So much for the history of the place. Getting there was sticky. There was one bus travelling once a day to Castrojeriz. This caused me to hire a taxi.

On arrival I found an hotel – not one that was in my guidebook – but a pleasant establishment and centrally located in this village. Village? Well, the place is categorised as a town but with a population of just 800 or so souls I reckon the term 'village' is more appropriate. That guidebook – again – describes the inhabitants as 'being permanently in siesta'. I found the opposite to be the case, with the locals proving to be a lively crew.

The castle, notwithstanding that it was a ruin looked an impressive structure, towering over the township. Then I discovered the guidebook had neglected to inform its reader that the castle was closed to visitors! No guide! Where was Abel when I needed him? However, there proved to be a number of signs about the place giving details of the function of various parts of the original building. It became abundantly clear that I did need that walking stick of mine.

At the end of my tour, I found myself on a route that was signed as pointing towards a 'taberna'. Even to one who didn't speak the language that had to be a bistro of some sort. Right? But suddenly the sky turned dark and grey and, as if to spite my new sun hat, it began to rain. How many days left? One hundred and sixty-two!

I had to get out of the rain. I discovered that I had at least got the meaning of taberna right, but travelling as fast as I could, there was no sign of a bistro or any such establishment along the path I'd taken. In fact, I eventually found myself back in the township. Damp as I was I settled into a bistro on the village square and had a restorative glass of red wine. Oh, all right! Two or three glasses of wine! The rain had by now stopped and I made my way back to my hotel.

That evening, I opted to dine in the hotel's pleasantly appointed dining room. No sooner had I settled myself and perused the menu from behind a glass of wine, than a group of some thirty or so chattering Americans arrived and accommodated themselves at the few tables that were vacant in the dining room. I was taken by the unkind thought as to just how many of these people were attempting to pass themselves off as Canadians when they are on their own and not part of a distinctive group.

There was no escaping the fact that the two waiters in the dining room had their hands full dealing with this group, and I had to wait a full half-hour before I had my order taken. However, the food when it arrived was excellent, and I received a courtesy bottle of wine. That went quite a way to making the wait worth it.

While I'd come to Castrojeriz to view the ruins of the castle, I had discovered there was, just three kilometres down the road another ruin; the old hospital of San Antón. There you have it, a walk in the morning.

What remains of the San Antón hospital is a sprawling ruin. It is nonetheless breathtaking in its size. There are a number of windows intact, and the interior decorations feature a tau cross; a tee shaped cross associated with Saint Francis of Assisi and an emblem much used by the Franciscans. Saint Francis supposedly passed this way, though just why I couldn't ascertain!

A number of infirm pilgrims heading for Santiago passed this way and are recorded as having received treatment at this hospital cum hospice. The place came to build a reputation as having personnel at the place who were proficient at treating the disease known as Saint Antony's Fire.

As a layman I can claim to know of two infections going by the name – Saint Anthony's Fire. One resulted in a painful inflammation of the skin. The other resulted in the mummification and gangrene of the limbs. Just which of these maladies was treated at San Antón I was unable to discover. Maybe both!

Satisfied with what I had seen I headed back to the hotel, or so I thought! I managed, again, to get myself lost! This became obvious when I came upon an ancient building that I had not passed on my way to San Antón's Hospital. A notice, at what I took to be the entrance to this old complex, told me I had chanced upon the Convent of the order of Saint Clare. The home of an order of Franciscan nuns.

Inside the entrance to the convent there stood what looked very like an empty alcove. Had it once housed a statue or a holy picture? As I gazed, puzzled by the abandoned alcove, I was passed by an elderly lady who knocked on the rebate. The space seemed to quickly open and the lady became the proud possessor of a sweet cake. Money was then placed on a tray and vanished into the depth.

I cogitated for a few moments on what I'd seen and clumsily described. I then realised that what I had taken as being an abandoned alcove turned out in fact to be a serving hatch or pass-through. Come to think of it I'd seen one or two in old houses in Ballarat. If there was a sister on the other side of the wall, dispensing cooked delicacies, then she was at a safe remove from any direct contact with the laity – though sensibly prepared to accept 'contaminated' cash for the sale. Of course! I realised the Poor Clare's are an enclosed order.

Since I was in the convent grounds, and no one had appeared to impede my progress, I meandered through the cloister and further investigation brought me to the convent chapel. Beautiful, uncluttered and quiet.

I could see several sisters in a segregated and gated choir off to the side of the high altar where the Blessed Sacrament was exposed in a richly jewelled monstrance. A number of tall stained-glass windows lit the apse. In one there was a depiction of the lily of the valley, another featured a rose. There was a rather gruesome window showing the stigmata and one with a monogram of AM, which I took to represent the term Ave Maria.

Apart from the monstrance standing above the high altar that edifice was adorned with a beautifully gilded tabernacle which gave the appearance of being supported by two angels. How splendid. I sat and let the quietude and beauty of the chapel sweep over me.

Ah well, so much for that contemplative time. It was now back to the hotel at Castrojeriz, and hopefully not getting lost this time. Tomorrow I intended to travel to Leon.

Leon

GETTING TO LEON PROVED A trial. It started with a three-hour bus trip. In the first instance I became convinced the driver was taking every backroad he could find, but, in spite of this we finally arrived in Burgos. Burgos! But I'd been here before. We were backtracking in every sense of the word. It was patiently explained to me by the driver – in broken English – that the only bus service to Leon departed from Burgos. Why hadn't I been told this earlier?

Finally, having got on the bus that was to take me to Leon, I arrived just in time to book myself into the Hotel La Pasada Regia in the centre of town. This proved to be a reconstructed and redecorated old 14th century building. It was surprisingly pleasant and the room I had proved very comfortable. Well, I would start in my 'tourist' role the next day.

I've mentioned before, haven't I, that many would now consider me as taking a pilgrim role, after all a lot of the places I'd been to were part of the Camino de Santiago. What a thought.

Next day, after a hearty breakfast, and having resisted the temptation to have champagne as my morning beverage, I went to view the town's famous cathedral. Easier said than done. Arriving at the cathedral I found myself at the end of a large queue of tourists and pilgrims waiting to get into the site. Pilgrims? It was easy to recognise them by their backpacks, hiking poles and, of course, the yellow and blue scallop pilgrim badge they wore.

Let me stop for a moment. You see, I've repeatedly had trouble with the identification of places as villages, towns and cities. Having finally, in desperation, availed myself of one of the internet facilities along the way, I discovered that the Spanish give every indication of having the same sort of trouble! The best I could come up with was the definition of a village simply as a small settlement, an *aidea*. A town, *pueblo*, apparently is a place claiming a population of 5,000 to 10,000. And finally, the identification as a city, a *ciudad*, can be granted to any place where the population exceeds 10,000. No doubt I'll still get it wrong! Back to where I was.

Receiving a nod and a wink from one of the cathedral attendants, I was extracted from the mob and taken to the establishment's museum. Why I was singled out from the crowd I have no real idea. It may have had something to do with my new hat and old walking stick. Or it could well have been that it was sensed that such a religious collection would have had no interest for the mob I'd seen at the cathedral entrance. Whatever. I got to view a wonderful collection of ecclesiastical artefacts and vestments. After this I wandered off to the old chapel, again apparently, a place of no interest to the pilgrim/tourist crowd.

Satisfied with all I'd seen, I made my way back to the hotel for a mid-day meal, after which I meandered into the township and went on a tour of the half-dozen churches that were open to visitors. It was in a Franciscan chapel that I came across the statue of a black Jesus. I'd never seen the likes of this. There was no one about to enlighten me. It was something I'd have to follow up. I left disappointed.

Later that evening in one of the side streets of Leon I came across a print shop. That took my interest, as I'd always fancied myself as something of an artist. When I entered, the gentleman I took to be the proprietor immediately spotted me as a 'foreigner'. It seemed he was the creator of all the present art and he pressed me to buy one of his prints. He explained, as best I could make out, in a mixture of Spanish and English how the Pope was already the proud (?) possessor of one of his prints. In order to make my escape I purchased a print, which I was informed was that of King David playing a lyre. It was rather attractive and cost a mere thirty euros.

Then, as opposed to making the quick getaway I had intended, I asked about the statue of Black Jesus I'd seen earlier in the day. The shop owner immediately took me to a back room where he produced a predominantly black costume with black cone shaped headgear, not unlike the Klu Klux Klan's head piece. He explained he was a member of a fraternity dedicated to the veneration of the Black Jesus.

"Why?" I asked.

Now his command of English was being stretched. As I best understood it, it had something to do with Spain's colonial past. My further questioning was met with a shrug. The annual procession which saw the statue of the Black Jesus carried aloft by costumed society members, well, that seemed to have been the fraternity's main attraction. At this point I let the matter rest and departed clutching my King David print.

That night I again dined at my hotel. As a precursor to the meal I sampled the local distillate, orujo. This spirit is made from wine skins and has an alcoholic content of some fifty per cent. Now, *that* I enjoyed.

The following morning, having been told about the city walls, I decided to take a walk along these ancient structures. The original walls were built in Roman times with later medieval brickwork added to augment the city's defences. I was told, by a helpful tourist, that there was an inscribed Roman brick held on display, somewhere, though he did not know exactly where this relic was, or what the inscription on it said. Not really helpful!

After I left the city walls I discovered, within a short walk, the Mother House of the Knights of Santiago. Part of this monastic building had been taken over by the State and converted into a parador. It was easy to access the place.

The Knights had been established to provide protection for the pilgrims crossing the main river into the emerging city of Leon. They then took to offering protection to these pilgrims as they passed along the particular route from Leon leading to Santiago.

Over the centuries the Knights have had a

fluid recent history. The Order was suppressed on the institution of the First Republic in 1873. Later restored they were, however, again suppressed at the creation of the Second Republic in 1931. The fall of this second republican institution again saw the Knights restored. Though few in number in Leon they are not short of lay members of the Order.

The priestly branch of the Knights' wear a distinctively marked vestment, which displays the Cross of St James. It is a red cross, the stem of which resembles a sword blade, and the handle displaying a *fleur-de-lis* emblem.

I was shown the parador accommodation offered at the monastery. I have to admit that I was anticipating I would be led into a monk-like chamber. Wrong! Even allowing for some modern alterations, it was clear that the Knights did, and probably still do, enjoy a particular level of comfort. It took very little to bring their accommodation up to parador standard.

My visit concluded it was back to the hotel.

The Hotel Pasada La Regina where I lodged, provided food of such a high standard that again I opted to dine there rather than giving my patronage to one of the local bistros.

Having digested the entrée and the main course, I was delighting in the taste of my *crema catalana* – a custard dish topped with caramelised sugar – when a group of six French tourists entered the dining room. Tourists? There was no sign of knapsacks, walking poles or the distinctive pilgrims' badge. French? Their loud conversation and accents gave them away.

The gentleman, who appeared to be the patron of the group evidently had no Spanish at his command and, being French, he wasn't going to be caught dead using English, even though there was an English language menu available. So, he ordered a meal for the group using a Spanish carta for reference.

The group were now into their fourth bottle of wine when the meal arrived. Clearly the patron was nonplussed by the dish they had been served. I had taken the opportunity to look at the Spanish and English menu cards. What had been ordered was *cazón en adobo*, or to describe the dish in English, deep fried shark. For a start, the French avoid this fish. The patron's reaction gave every indication that he considered his plate to contain a creature from outer space. So much for that Frenchman's epicurean knowledge.

The next day I was set to move on from Leon. It was my intention to travel to the Hospital de Orbigo. I would reach my destination by bus, and I hoped the driver taking me out of the city would take a route that avoided taking the bus through the unattractive modern suburbs and circumvent the industrial sites that had presented such an unattractive preface to ancient Leon.

Fortunately, the driver was of the same mind as myself, or else his employers had devised a way out of the city that avoided all the architectural monstrosities which had upset me on my arrival.

A Whimsical Journey

Hospital de Orbigo

ORBIGO IS A TOWN OF just 1,000 inhabitants. I suppose that actually makes it a village! The locals boast they have the longest medieval bridge in Spain. The Ministry of Culture, or some such unthinking body, sponsored the 'refurbishment' of the bridge with the resulting 'Disneyfication' of the structure, so that it is illuminated by lights built into its masonry.

Anyone coming to the bridge from the Leon side – like myself – will be greeted by a balconied building flaunting red plastic chairs and tables, sponsored by Mathou beer, and in addition an ugly yellow and black sign proclaiming the building as an 'Hostal'.

A Whimsical Journey

I had no intention of giving my patronage to such a monstrous place. Fortunately, shortly after this introduction to the township I came across a small parador which sported a neat fish pond, oh, and a resident black cat. I quickly discovered I was the only guest. That was fine by me!

But the bridge was what had drawn me to Orbigo. Built in the 15th century, it was a structure of some 200 metres in length. It constituted the main thoroughfare for those wanting to get to Santiago. In 1434, Don Suero de Quinones, together with fellow knights, took control of the bridge and challenged any other knight who wanted to cross it.

Well, I knew about Don Suero and his actions regarding the bridge, but what was all that fuss about? A challenge to strange knights and such? Once again that guidebook came to the rescue. The bridge had become a feature in a love story!

Don Suero had fallen in love with the beautiful Donna Leonor de Tobar, but the lady did not return his affection. As a consequence

A Whimsical Journey

of this rejection Don Suero took to wearing a heavy iron collar every Thursday and fasting. Oh, what love can do to a man!

It was then that Don Suero gathered some nine or ten of his companions and vowed to challenge any other knight who wished to cross the bridge over the Orbigo River. Such chivalric jousts would continue until three hundred lances had been broken.

This was all well and good, except that Don Suero and his companion knights had become incapacitated by wounds before this figure of one thousand broken lances could be reached. The affair of the bridge was over.

As it turned out, Donna Leonor was so impressed by the Don's action that she took to returning his affection with the result that the pair were married.

When he came to hear of it, King Juan II of Castile was so impressed by the whole affair that he arranged for stands to be erected to accommodate spectators and he declared that jousting was to be an annual event at the bridge.

As it was, I'd arrived too late to witness this jousting re-enactment. But I'd seen the bridge, decorated as it was. That was enough. To be honest Orbigo had turned out to be something of a disappointment.

The town of Astorga was just down the road from Orbigo. I'd get a bus there tomorrow.

Astorga

ON MY ARRIVAL IN THIS town of 10,000 souls I wandered about the place and admired its compact medieval layout. It was the Bishop's Palace that caught my attention. It was an Antoni Gaudi building. The exterior gave the appearance of being, in part, ancient and modern. How much of this was Gaudi's doing? I'd find out more about that later.

The building was started in 1890, this after the original palace had been destroyed by fire. Gaudi was approached by Bishop Grau and was asked to undertake the design of a new palace. The bishop and Gaudi were old acquaintances.

A Whimsical Journey

There can be little doubt that initially Gaudi enthusiastically undertook the commission. He produced some magnificent tile work and created beautifully incised ceiling decorations.

Before work on the building was finished, Bishop Grau died. With the palace still a work in progress the diocesan council decided to take over the supervision of the completion of the building. Gaudi, use to working at his own pace and improvising as he went along, abandoned the undertaking. This possibly explains the palace's strange exterior.

In consequence the work on the building was not completed until 1915 *and* without the help of Gaudi. Further, the palace was never occupied by a bishop and now houses a museum.

I needed to find an hotel, and there it was – The Hotel Gaudi. Was there no getting away from the man? But, on enquiry I found that the only connection between Antoni Gaudi and the hotel was in the use of his name. It was a place endowed with a striking – some would say strange? – exterior. It did have the advantage of being within walking distance of the local cathedral of Saint Mary, sometime in the past declared a national monument. Buildings ecclesiastical again!

When I got to the cathedral it proved to be an imposing and solid piece of architecture. Once inside I was taken by surprise because there was no immediate sight of the high altar. Where had that centre piece gotten to? Eventually it came into view once I had travelled down a side ambulatory. It struck me that the local clergy were of the view that the altar was there for them – if laity chanced on it, all well and good! But then, who am I to be critical of such things?

There were a few small groups being led about by guides. Maybe I would have been better served – and more appreciative of the cathedral had I joined one of those groups.

There were still the old city walls to be visited. They had been built by the Romans so as to defend the emerging township. Over two kilometres long, I found myself swaggering along the walk at the top of the walls. In my imagination I was a Roman soldier. What fancy does for one. Where had that vertigo gone?

Now, having become Romanised, so to speak, I broke a rule, and joined a guided tour that was to view all the old Roman sites in Astorga. This walk took me through the Roman remains that were to be found about the town. The Romans had certainly made an effort to establish themselves in this part of the world. We visited the site of the Tenth Gemina Legion. If my school history served me, the Tenth were a mob that Julius Caesar had used during his invasion of Gaul. We were shown their sewer system. I knew that at least the upper-class Romans were a hygienic lot – hot baths, toilets. Again those history lessons. And finally, we were shown a *domus*, which went some of the way towards supporting what I've just written! All very satisfying.

The next day I had set myself to journey to Ponferrada.

A Whimsical Journey

Molinaseca and Ponferrada

I HAD WORKED OUT IT would be interesting to take a bus first to the village of Molinaseca, have a quick look about the place, with a visit to the 'Roman Bridge' and then go onward to Ponferrada. Oh, how the best laid plans can 'gan aft agly'.

For a start I was later to discover the so-called 'Roman Bridge' was a medieval seven arched structure over the Meruleo River. I believe the river sports an abundance of trout. Hemingway, where were you?

The bridge, a feature of the village, seemed to have had a great deal of medieval work done on it. I began to have suspicions that it wasn't quite what it was made out to be, viz. Roman. For all of that it was certainly a more attractive structure than that Disneyfied travesty I'd left behind at Hospital de Ordigo.

It was then I realised I'd spent so much time on this visit that I had missed the last bus heading for Ponferrada. I would have to stay the night in Molinaseca. Rather than hunt for an hotel I identified a group of pilgrims; back packs, walking poles, badges, etc. etc., and I followed them to the local Albergue Compestela. I, of course, couldn't claim to be a pilgrim, but, in this instance, I wasn't asked if I was, and I didn't offer the information that I wasn't!

It proved a very good place to sleep. However, things took a turn for the worst in the morning.

Breakfast was a simple affair; all the guests were sat at a communal table. That in itself proved no great problem, in fact it was rather comfortable, but a few places down the board there was an annoyingly sharp voiced female holding loud court in English for a group of pilgrims. From the little I could make out of what she had to say, she was relating the history of all the various places along the Camino de Santiago. It was obvious from the expressions of group they had no real idea just what the lady was on about. A guide in control of a group of unfortunates? Or maybe she was a lady taken by her own opinion on everything and was convinced others would like to hear from her. This address – if that is the right word – continued long enough to enable the party to finish their breakfasts and make a hasty joint exit. In the quietness that followed I allowed myself another cup of coffee.

As I sat sipping my fresh brew *that* lady, having pro tem, been abandoned by her group of pilgrims, cornered a number of Americans and, having introduced herself to them as a countrywoman began to tell them all about the Camino!

The group she was now haranguing had less patience than her missing pilgrims. They simply got up from the table and left. In a flash the lady got herself sat down on a vacant chair next to me.

She was proving worse for loudness and persistence than any tourist/pilgrim guide I had so far come across. I quickly realised there was only one way I could make my escape. I used the one scrap of Spanish I had at my command. As she started by introducing herself and demanding my name, I looked her in the eye, smiled and declared, "No hablo Engles." Then I rose and with a bow, made my swift departure.

Last evening, having arrived by bus to Molinaseca, and then discovering there was no regular service to Ponferrada I opted to travel to that destination by taxi! Better sure than sorry, eh?

Ponferrada took its name from the fact that the town had a bridge which the local bishop, back in the 11th century, had constructed. His intention was to ease the passage of those pilgrims who were making their way to Santiago. It was a wooden bridge constructed over the River Sil. Later the bridge was reinforced with iron struts, and it was then the place became known as Ponferrada, or to revert to my shaky Latin, *Pons Ferrata*.

Aside from the bridge one of the attractions

of the place was the Castle of the Knights Templar or, to grant them their full title, which I only later learnt: Poor Fellow Soldiers of Christ and the Temple of Solomon.

In 1204 King Alfonso IX of Leon and Galacia gave the town to the Templars in return for their support. The Knights themselves, as a Catholic Order, protected the northern borders of Spain against incursions of the southern conquering Muslims.

The Templars' castle is now owned by the King of Spain. While the exterior of the castle is well preserved there is little of the original interior remaining. There is some compensation to be found inside the modern facilities by a number of displays featuring the township's history. There is also a display of 'reconstructed' period costumes. All tastefully done and interesting. Then there was the Templars' library. What a startling display of books and manuscripts. The Irish, I know, carry on about their Book of Kells – they should come and have a look at the literary material available at Ponferrada.

I wasn't going to search for an albergue, and had booked myself into a local hotel, named Hotel Temple Ponferrada. The place had nothing to do with the Templars, but a catchy name, nonetheless. The hotel does bill itself as medievally themed; maybe that accounts for the Temple title!

At dinner that night I ordered Morcilla sausage from the hotel's dining room menu.

Morcilla sausage? Live dangerously!

On brief research the dish seems to be related in some small way to Scottish haggis. I know it is a noble aspiration to see that nothing of a beast, slain to feed us, is let go to waste. For example, when the pig is considered there is of course bacon, liver and so on. In fact, the Irish go as far as eating the beast's feet – a fact they choose to disguise by presenting the dish under the appellation of *crubeens* – I've been told the real spelling in Irish is crúibín, meaning simply pig's trotter. There's that Seán influence again with those *fadas*.

For their part, the Scots use the pig's minced intestines and by throwing in a handful of oatmeal, and playing the bagpipes, attempt to distract attention from what is being served.

But then, perhaps, I was just being singularly insular. It could well be that some of our Australian dishes would fall foul of a similar culinary investigation.

The morcilla I was served was a delicious blood sausage, flavoured with onion and spices and a touch of rice. It was delicious. No need for bagpipes, or the *fada*!

Next stop, Villafranca.

A Whimsical Journey

Villafranca del Bierzo

NEXT I WENT TO VILLAFRANCA by bus. The town is just over twenty-five kilometres away from Ponferrada, so there was no way I was going to attempt a walk.

On arrival I booked into the Casa Rural, a delightful, renovated 17th century establishment.

Just to digress for a moment. I have to admit that travel fatigue was setting in, so I decided that the rest of my time in Spain would consist more of *stop* than *go*. To be honest I had come to set my sights on Santiago.

And, on a totally different subject, I have to

allow that the meals in Spain had, to my appetite, frequently proved the equivalent of a whole day's eating. So, in anticipation of this, on my first night at the hotel I ordered a salad. If it proved to be a surprisingly *small* meal, I could always order a dessert. As it was, the white bean salad I ordered was enough, consisting of the beans, tomato olives and smoked paprika!

Back to the township.

During my visit to Villafranca I was able to walk round the exterior of the Palacio de los Marqueses. It was a very large rectangular building with a tall circular tower at each of its corners. It had more the appearance of a fortified residence than a palace. The palace had been built in the 16th century and occupied over the years by various nobles. Now it was privately owned, and the interior of the place/palace could only be viewed with the permission of the owner. Who was the owner? The locals appeared unsure, or unwilling to name him, or her. I certainly was disinclined to attempt tracking them down. I moved on.

There are a goodly number of churches in

Villafranca. The one I was most interested to see was the Church of Saint James. There is a door on the north side of this church known as the Door of Forgiveness. If one were sick, injured, or in any way certifiably unwell you could obtain an indulgence or forgiveness as if you'd completed the Camino de Santiago. I couldn't come to a complete understanding of the terms one had to meet before qualifying for this 'exemption', so I'd settle for making it on to Santiago de Compostela itself.

On the subject of churches, only three of these establishments are connected to holy orders: the Franciscans, the Clare Sisters and the Pauline Fathers. I've already visited establishments of the first two orders, but the Pauline Fathers? Well, their monastery still stands, but it is now run as a hostelry for pilgrims and tourists, together with a museum and an eatery. Truth to tell I had in mind something a little more ecclesiastical.

When I got back to the Casa Rural where I was staying I was approached by a fellow guest. A tall, clean-shaven and well turned-out young man, wearing summery clothes and sporting a light tan. Spanish?

He greeted me in English and invited himself to join me. "You look English," he declared, "and I would love to have a chat with you."

Me, looking English? What would my Irish ancestors say to that? And as a fully established Australian to boot. I was initially tempted to use that 'no hablo Engles' ploy, but tact and kindness kept me quiet. He introduced himself as Jeffrey Clark. It transpired that the man's father was English and his mother Scottish. He was born in Edinburgh but spent his life in London. The past few years he had lived in Argentina where he bred cattle. "Argentina?" I asked.

"Yes," came his reply. "I always fancied cattle."

"But why Argentina?" I wanted to know.

"Why not?" His parents spoke only English, and his Spanish was, by his own admission, marginal. So be it.

In turn I told Jeffrey how I'd set my sights on getting to Santiago. He told me of his intention also to get to Santiago, but he proposed to spend a few days in Villafranca. Interesting as Jeffrey was, I was pleased that I wasn't going to be lumbered with a travelling companion as I went on my way.

My guidebook – again – gave me details of Lugo, an old Roman city located off the way to Santiago, but, perhaps, worth a visit. I opted to stay with the decision I'd already made. Santiago it was to be.

Later, I enquired of the management how best to get to Santiago. I was told that there would be a bus leaving for my destination the following evening, provided the management informed the bus company that there was a passenger waiting for them. "We have a bus station, but the bus doesn't stop here unless requested," Ermingo, the Casa Rural manager informed me. "I will phone the bus company," went on Ermingo.

Then, to top it all, he booked me into an hotel in Santiago. "It is in the old city," he assured me. "And no more than 600 metres from the cathedral."

The bus would collect me at three p.m. the next day. So, after breakfast the next morning I made my way to Clare Sisters Church. The convent garden sported a cypress tree which the locals claimed was at least 400 years old. I was also told it was the largest and oldest in the whole of Spain. Who was I to argue with the *facts*?

When I sought to enter the convent church I found it was locked. Frustrating! By now it was time to make my way to the bus station. Santiago here I come!

A Whimsical Journey

Santiago

THE BUS DRIVER CAUTIOUSLY CHECKED his passenger list and, finding my name, pointed me to the only remaining seat on the packed vehicle. The journey to Santiago took three and a half uncomfortable hours.

Earlier, back at the Casa Rural, Ermingo had booked me into an hotel in Santiago. "Part of the service," he had boasted. He had assured me the accommodation was no more than 600 metres from the cathedral. Well, that was a calculation clearly made on the basic assumption that I was a bloody crow and could fly from point A to B directly!

When I arrived at the hotel I immediately

realised that the place was going to lose my patronage. I spent an unsatisfactory night in the hotel. The next morning, I informed reception I had received an urgent message that I had to return immediately to Australia. This whopper would have been exposed if I'd been asked, as a point of interest, to show the mobile phone by which I had received a transmission in this 'poorly located' part of the world.

Later I secured a room on the Rua do Vilar, right in the medieval city centre. It was a double room with a balcony providing an unobstructed view of the cathedral. Now that I was in Santiago, hefting my trusty walking stick, I set off to see the reliquary of Saint James. My stout walking stick was viewed by many as a weapon and my passage to the cathedral was unimpeded by the crowds of tourists and pilgrims who scattered on my approach and provided me with unimpeded passage to my destination.

When I entered the cathedral I was confronted by a long queue waiting to ascend the high altar and embrace the gilded statue of Saint James displayed there. I hate queues!

A Whimsical Journey

I settled for examining the giant thurible suspended from the ceiling and which swung across the nave from the north to the south transept. The thurible is handled by eight red-robed men, and they are described as *tiraboleiros*. That I can hardly pronounce let alone know exactly what the title means. I was told that the thurible was swung on high feasts and holidays. Its declared religious purpose being to dispel malignant and evil spirits. However, I did hear from other sources that, in medieval times, it originally served the function of fumigating the transepts and covered the stench of the travel worn, unclean and unwashed pilgrims. I prefer this explanation – it strikes me as being nearer the truth regarding the thurible's original purpose.

Having now seen the inside of the cathedral, I realised I'd have to return if I wished to touch the relic of Saint James; leastways get up close to the gilded statue on the high altar. I set off to visit the old shops which I believed stood all around the cathedral. This turned out to be something of a disappointment. I had imagined how, as in the old times, there would still be silversmiths and pilgrim shops all about the place, but the place had been given over to modern souvenir shops and stalls.

I decided to make my way further afield, but the trek away from the old city centre brought me up against modern supermarkets and heavy motor traffic. I quickly made my way back the way I'd come. You can imagine my surprise when I discovered that during the time I had been away the whole courtyard in front of the cathedral had become filled with motor vehicles. All the cars were vintage vehicles – Aston Martins, Morgans, Triumphs and a Rolls Royce. All British and not a French, Italian, Swedish or Spanish vehicle to be seen. I later learnt that Santiago was the destination for many car rallies. Obviously, I had been witness to a veteran British rally. In front of the cathedral! Come to think of it, a lovely mix of the secular and sacred.

The hectic day ended with a meal at one of the local bistros where I found myself surrounded by fellow diners of all nationalities. I could only assume there were as many tourists as pilgrims present among the lot.

Back in the hotel and safely abed I was woken from a sound sleep at three in the morning by a noisy mob of young students from the local university. They had been celebrating the end of their exams. Then again in the early hours of the morning – well, I reckon it was about eight o'clock – a group of boisterous pilgrims, having completed the Camino, were loudly 'signing-in'; having their documents stamped at the office across the road from the hotel. So much for a holiday lie-in, instead I was going to have an early morning breakfast.

I had already decided that this was to be my last day in Santiago, so what was left to be seen or done? For a start I had to touch the relic of Saint James. I couldn't very well tell people I'd been to Santiago and not done the honours at Saint James's reliquary. But there's a thought. Was that gilded statue above the high altar a reliquary? I'd have to make enquiries. That could be done later.

Then, down the road from the hotel there

was Café Casino. My guidebook – again that helpful piece of literature – told me that the café was built in 1873 and was a venue frequented by the high society of this part of the world. As one professing to be interested in social history, I had to visit this venue to see how it measured up to our gold-rush architecture back in Ballarat.

Café Casino? For a start there was no evidence that the place ever functioned as a casino. Admittedly there was a sense of the British Victorian about the place - well, it was built when Queen Victoria was on the throne in the UK - but I was of the opinion that Ballarat still rated as the example par excellence of décor of the period. Well, at least I'd seen the place, now for the cathedral and Saint James.

Questions asked at the hotel had led me to the discovery that the gilded statue at the high altar was not the reliquary of Saint James. His coffin was down in a crypt *under* the altar. The long queue I'd witnessed the previous day was, apparently, made up of pilgrims wishing to embrace the life-sized statue of Saint James, in an act intended to show gratitude for a successful journey and a pilgrimage completed.

It was afternoon when I got to the cathedral. The place was surprisingly quiet with very few patrons, or should that be pilgrims? There was no evidence of a queue pressing to get to *that* gilded statue. I had been told that there was a set of steps behind the altar leading down into a crypt and there I would find the remains of Saint James contained in a decorated silver coffin. If I desired I would have the opportunity to kneel at a *prie-dieu* and have a word with the saint. Later I was to learn that the saint was not alone since two of his companions, Saint Athanasius and Saint Theodore were also interred with him. It seems Martin Luther had pessimistically remarked concerning the remains in the shrine: "Who knows if there isn't just a dead dog buried there? Or a dead horse?" Scepticism is a wonderful attribute, isn't it.

A Whimsical Journey

Leaving

I HAD DECIDED I WAS going to leave Santiago by train back to Madrid. To my way of thinking the flight from Madrid to Melbourne would be enough time spent in the air, and the train trip would be something of a novelty, particularly since the journey was to be made on a bullet train. I was told the machine could travel at close to 300 kilometres per hour – that's something like 187 miles per hour in the old measurement.

The experience proved to be terrific. I had my own cabin, and while the trip was to be no more than four hours I had time to get a meal at the café and a few drinks at the bar.

A Whimsical Journey

There was no direct flight from Madrid to Melbourne, but that was fine by me. I needed lots of time to wind-down and collect my thoughts with regard to my experience in Spain. Cathay Pacific would get me to Hong Kong then I'd connect with Qantas.

All went smoothly.

When I got back to Ballarat I'd have tales to tell Jane and Clive. Yes, some of the guides I'd encountered were great and some were – for want of a better word – indifferent. But then, in my few previous journeys I never had to rely on guides, so who am I to make comments?

I'd bought a gift for Jane and Clive. A scallop shell bracelet for her and a keyring for Clive. Yes, I know they were symbolic for a pilgrimage completed, but I have to admit, by the end of the trip up north, I had come, to a degree, to consider myself a pilgrim, particularly after that Saint James business in Santiago.

Who knows, with the right equipment, say a couple to trekking poles, decent walking shoes, and a great deal of time, I may well go back as a proper pilgrim ... staying at albergues along the way.

Maybe.

A Whimsical Journey

Sometime later

Yes, I'd decided to let the public have my diary, or more correctly, the small book I'd written, relying on my diary entries.

I asked Jane if she would read the manuscript. She lectured on literature or some such, at the local university. She read the draft.

"I see you took a different route than me," she declared. She had, in fact, walked the Camino.

I agreed that was so. "I started the way Clive suggested. It seemed a reasonable idea." And I wandered about a little, but I said nothing about that.

Jane nodded. "Barcelona and then Madrid."

It was my turn to nod.

She waved the manuscript at me. "Your tenses are all over the place," she snapped.

"Entries from my diary," I said in my defence. "Some remarks were made early, others a day or two, later."

Who is worried about tenses? "Oh, all right, I'll tidy them up ... a little," I told her.

Jane harrumphed and laid down the manuscript. "I suppose it will do," she declared by way of indifferent acceptance.

"Good," was all I could manage.

So, here it is.

Also by the author

Two Fat Ladies and Hercules Tom:
The Story of the Australian Giant Family
Nkosi:
An African Adventure
As Your Worship Pleases:
Tales from a Magistrates' Court in Africa
Unholy Orders
The Experimental Gentleman:
Thomas Bungeelene 1846 – 1865
The Flying Pieman:
An Historical Adventure of
William Francis King 1807 – 1873
The Last Drop
The Hangman's Story
Michael Gately 1822 — 1883
A Whimsical Journey Through the North of Spain

Victorian Crime Titles:
An Eye for Murder
Murder in Victorian Melbourne.
For Love Or Money
Crime in Victorian Melbourne
Four Bodies and a Box
Murder in Victorian Melbourne
The Body in the Cellar
Murder in Victorian Melbourne

Children's Titles:
Simus the Stone
The Mysterious Forest
The Thirteen Treasures
The Old Man and the Dragon
The Bear Facts
Out and About
Heaven Above
Rough Diamonds

www.ingramcontent.com/pod-product-compliance
Lightning Source LLC
Chambersburg PA
CBHW022305060426
42446CB00007BA/595